ISRAEL
A FIRST VIEW

SNOWDON

Foreword by John Mortimer, captions by Gemma Levine

LITTLE, BROWN AND COMPANY BOSTON TORONTO

The photographs for this book were taken in
Israel and in the Israel Military Zone

Designer: Paul Bowden

First American edition

First published in Great Britain in 1986

This book was produced by
George Weidenfeld and Nicolson Limited

Printed and bound in Italy

Library of Congress Cataloging-in-Publication Data

Snowdon, Antony Armstrong-Jones, Earl of, 1930–
    Israel. A First View.

    1. Israel—Description and travel—Views.   I. Title.
DS108.5.S58 1986   956.94′054   85–23891
ISBN 0–316–80226–3

FOREWORD

John Mortimer

Five days is the average length of a visit by a tourist to Israel. It may not seem a great deal of time to devote to a history which goes back to the sixteenth century before Christ, when the people of that country worshipped a large number of idols in stone-carved temples and the nomad Ivrim, the Hebrews, crossed the Euphrates into the land of Canaan. Five days may seem a brief tribute to a land in which the great religious ideas of the western world have fought, suffered, struggled for existence or lived more or less easily together. Jews, Romans, Hellenes, Christians, Arabs and Turks have left their monuments and bloodstains on the landscape of a country which can be flown across in a few minutes. It's the land of Jesus and Moses, King David and King Herod, Richard the Lionheart, Nebuchadnezzar and Golda Meir. Even to think about such matters, to contemplate such characters, would seem an impossible undertaking in five days. The latest invaders of Israel, the packaged tourists bumping off to Galilee in their buses or wandering, bemused, round the old city of Jerusalem, may be thought to take away only a superficial view of this extraordinary country which occupies the Middle East like a sign of courage and a never ceasing argument.

And yet there is a great deal to be said for an instant experience. First impressions, like love at first sight, may be deeper and more reliable than a lifetime's acquaintance. The advocate in the courtroom may have only a few minutes to assess the character of a witness or a juryman. Long lasting quarrels or friendships can begin with a fleeting insult or handshake. In five days there may be no time to gain a deep knowledge of a country but there is also no time for reverence. No one back from a five day tourist trip can possibly write purple prose about a place or describe it with that knowing and superior air which makes so many travel books intolerable. On a five day tour the eye takes in a million visual impressions, most of which will be discarded and only a few remain to be pasted in the album of memory. It was in this spirit that Snowdon went to Israel for five days and clicked his camera almost every time a tourist blinked. He had to work quickly because the Jewish and the Arab inhabitants have a deep mistrust of photographers. It's a collection of these quick glances that make up this book.

What do you remember of a country after five days? Perhaps not the sights that you are meant to carry away, the Cathedral or the Art Gallery, the new Housing Development or the remarkably laid out Public Gardens. You remember the awful drive from the airport, the dark little café by the ruins where you were at last able to go to the loo and two old men were singing as they played dominoes, the comically pretentious menu outside the grim restaurant by the railway station or the beautiful girl traffic cop hastily renewing her lipstick at the crossroads. I find it difficult to visualise the interior of St Peter's in Rome, but once, when I was there, a thirsty habitué took me to a little bar behind the high altar, the sight of which will be forever printed on my memory. It was a quiet and discreet place where the official guides and a few cleaning ladies were politely drinking Lacryma Christi. It would have been the perfect subject for a Snowdon photograph.

There seems to me to be a great deal of honesty in these pictures. Of all the manifestly untrue statements ever made the most misleading is that 'The camera cannot lie'. Clearly cameras are the most terrible liars, if they were not they would hardly be so popular with the advertising industry. Cameras not only lie about the size of hotel swimming pools, the casual elegance of clothes and the succulence of food, they can constantly be employed to make politicians look more likeable, actresses more beautiful and landscapes more spectacular than they ever are in real life. These pictures aren't at the service of any agency, nor do they state any political idea. They are simply what the eye of the camera saw, on a hot and airless plain or down a windy street. It caught sight of something comic, touching, bizarre or quite mundane, remembered it clearly for some reason and brought it home from the holiday.

The problem facing any collection of memories is knowing what to leave out. When they are memories of Israel the difficulty is increased by the extraordinary complexity and contradictions of the place. The dozen Jewish communities speak different languages, have different customs and colours. The majority of the Christians are Arabs and the Jewish Ministry of Tourism has a special department for Christian pilgrims. The most desirable women seem to be in the army or the police, and the people who produced some of the world's greatest artists, musicians and impressarios are compelled, in Israel, also to give birth to skilled soldiers and brilliant generals. When I went to attend a trial in Haifa I was grateful to find the Criminal Law of England applied so accurately, but I also discovered that most of the emergency powers assumed by the British Government to suppress the Haganah have been carefully preserved in the legal system of a freed Israel. The land which gave birth to a religion which announced the coming of peace and goodwill to mankind has been almost incessantly fought over, and among its bloodiest invaders were surely the Crusaders. All these contradictions, like the endless theological debates which vitalise the Jewish religion, no doubt make up the fascination of Israel.

Snowdon's pictures mix the past and the present. A plate of fish still waits to be divided, the fishing boat on the Sea of Galilee has been transformed into a concrete restaurant, the fishermen's nets are made of plastic, the carpenter is still there, building a staircase. Meanwhile the Wailing Wall is being wired by the telephone service, a tramp lies asleep on a bench in Rothschild Avenue, the Mayor of Jerusalem has a discussion with a tailor, the sweating young soldier passes a poster advertising erotic swimwear (bathing-suits are said to be among the best buys in Israel), a lady tourist covers her body with health-giving mud, young Rabbis collect old 78s from a pile in a street market, and the instant observer wonders what kind of music they are selecting. Out in the desert a telegraph pole provides a slender shade, a mule pulls a plough and the fields are cultivated as they might have been in the days of the prophet Elijah. At the bus station the soldiers are bored, yawning, tired out by an ever-disputed frontier, except for the one in love who is kissing his girlfriend goodbye.

The returning tourist may not have his memories as beautifully composed as these pictures. But if you or I were ever in Israel we had these glimpses of living also. It may take Snowdon's photographs to remind us of them.

ACKNOWLEDGEMENTS

The publishers would like to acknowledge the contribution made by Gemma Levine who initiated and has coordinated an exhibition of photographs of Israel which is to tour the United Kingdom between 1986 and 1988.

The photographs for this book were taken during a visit to Israel sponsored by the Bank Hapoalim B.M. in the United Kingdom under the management of Joseph Dauber. Some of these photographs together with others taken by different photographers will also form part of this exhibition.

Invaluable assistance was provided by Mayor Kollek and the Municipality of Jerusalem, Mrs Aviva Briskman and the Israeli Foreign Office, Kodak U.K. and Mr Benny Bitter, who acted as guide.

I would like to express my personal gratitude and thanks to Matthew Donaldson for his tireless assistance while on location, Terry Lack for printing the black and white photographs with such expertise, Evelyn Humphries for sorting out, organizing and filing transparencies, and in particular Paul Bowden for his impeccable care in choosing and laying out the photographs with such speed and talent.

SNOWDON

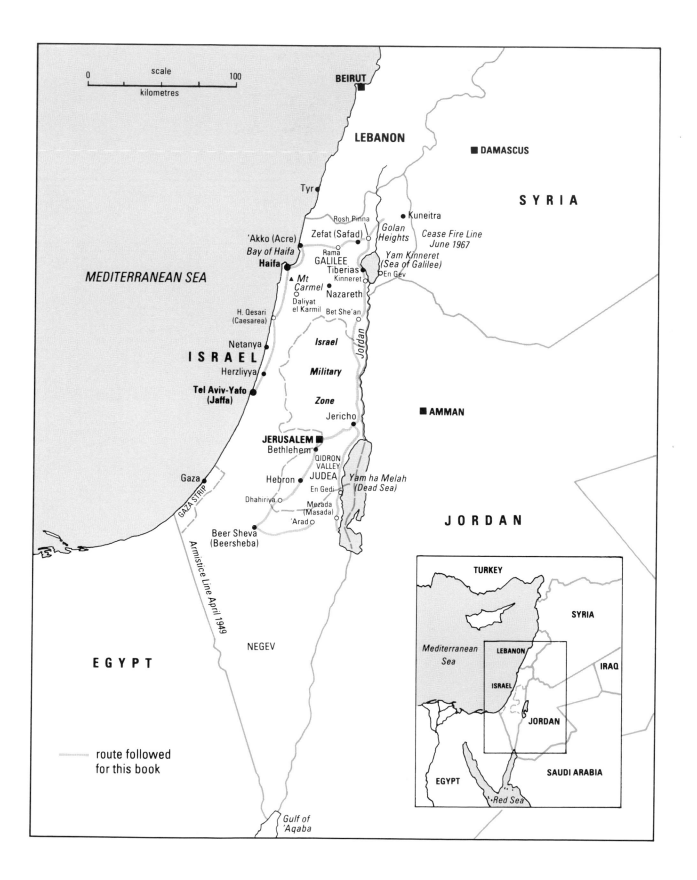

scale

0   100

kilometres

BEIRUT

LEBANON

■ **DAMASCUS**

Tyr

Rosh Pinna

Kuneitra

S Y R I A

'Akko (Acre)

Zefat (Safad)

Golan
Heights

Cease Fire Line
June 1967

Bay of Haifa

Rama

Yam Kinneret
(Sea of Galilee)

Haifa

GALILEE

Tiberias

En Gev

MEDITERRANEAN SEA

▲ Mt
Carmel

Kinneret

Daliyat
el Karmil

Nazareth

H. Qesari
(Caesarea)

Bet She'an

Jordan

Netanya

Israel

ISRAEL

Herzliyya

Military

Tel Aviv-Yafo
(Jaffa)

Zone

Jericho

■ **AMMAN**

JERUSALEM ■

Bethlehem

QIDRON
VALLEY

Gaza

JUDEA

Hebron

En Gedi

Yam ha Melah
(Dead Sea)

Dhahiriya

Mezada
(Masada)

J O R D A N

'Arad

Beer Sheva
(Beersheba)

Armistice Line April 1949

NEGEV

E G Y P T

route followed
for this book

Gulf of
'Aqaba

TURKEY

SYRIA

Mediterranean
Sea

LEBANON

IRAQ

ISRAEL

JORDAN

EGYPT

SAUDI ARABIA

·*Red Sea*

ISRAEL
A FIRST VIEW

Mayor Kollek with Mr Sammy Barsum
a tailor, the souk,
the Old City, Jerusalem

Israeli soldier, Petach Tikva Road, Tel Aviv

Waiting on the corner of Allenby and Hayarkon Street, Tel Aviv

Ploughing, Dhahiriya,
an Arab town south of Hebron

Bedouin, Beersheba market

Bedouin, Dabbeshet, near Arad

Sheep skins drying on an Arab balcony,
the port of Old Jaffa

Arab farmer at Beersheba, Thursday market

Mizpe Jericho

Tourists, Masada

Donkey in graveyard
(the Qidron Valley)
by the Mount of Olives

Workshop, Ha'aliya Hashnia Street, the port of Old Jaffa

Entrance to the Church of Nativity in Bethlehem

Praying at the Western Wall, Jerusalem

Electricians repairing communications by the Western Wall

Israeli soldiers,
the courtyard
of the Church
of the
Holy Sepulchre,
the Old City,
Jerusalem

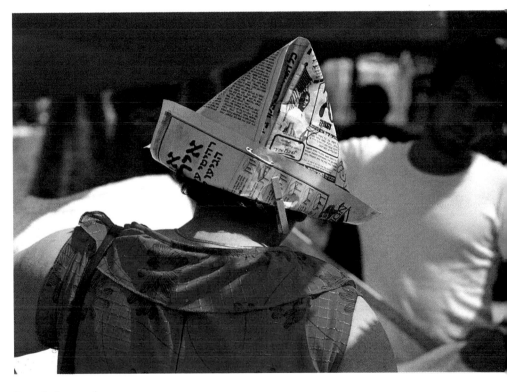

Beersheba market

Graffiti, the port of Old Jaffa

Five small fishes in the port of Acre

Concrete boat restaurant,
the Sea of Galilee

The Rothschild Boulevard, Tel Aviv

Wall, Hamigdalor Street, Jaffa

Shade, Omer near Beersheba

'Centre Bus Station', Hashomoron, Tel Aviv

Memorial to an attack on a Jewish bus,
the Rosh Pinnah–Safad road

42

Beersheba market

Tank scrap-yard, Beach Road, near Tel Aviv

Meron High Road, Galilee

Hayyé Adam Road, Mea She'arim, the religious quarter,
Jerusalem

Orthodox Jew, Mea She'arim

49

Mea She'arim

Mea She'arim Road

The Old City, Jerusalem

Street stall selling 78 r.p.m. records, Mea She'arim

En Gedi, by the Dead Sea

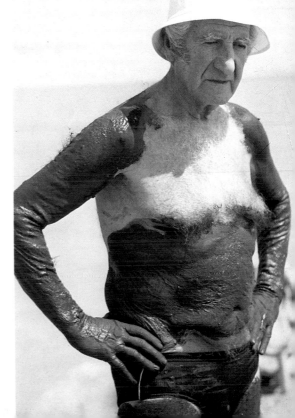

En Gedi

Jericho

Ethiopian monks in the
courtyard of the Church
of the Holy Sepulchre,
the Old City, Jerusalem

Ethiopian Jews, Safad

Bridal shop, Acre

A Druze bride,
Daliyat el Karmil
in the Carmel Mountains

Wedding photograph,
the park of Yemin Moshe,
Jerusalem

66

The Moslem Sheik, Abdul El Morti-El-Alami,
head of the El Hanka Mosque
in the Christian quarter of Jerusalem

Archbishop Dionysius Behuam Jajjawi,
the Syrian Orthodox Patriarchal Vicar
of the Holy Land and Jordan

Archbishop Athenasius, head of the Ethiopian Orthodox Church in Israel

Graffiti, the port of Old Jaffa

Ice cream parlour, Acre

Bedouins, the Negev near
Arad, east of Beersheba

74

The souk, the Old City,
Jerusalem

The Jewish market,
Jerusalem

The market, Jericho

Mea She'arim

By the Western Wall

Orthodox Jew celebrates his religious maturity (barmitzvah) by the Western Wall

Lubavich schoolchildren, Safad

Mashtodz Parilouysian, ninety-year-old priest
of the Armenian church, the hospices of Jerusalem

The 'Gate to the Shore', Acre

Orthodox Jew, Mea She'arim,
near the Western Wall

Druze woman, an olive grove on the Safad–Acre road, Rama

The bark of a 2,000-year-old olive tree

Carpenters making staircase,
the port of Old Jaffa

Chaim Ovadia, during the last twenty years
gardener to Foreign Minister Abba Eban
and Prime Ministers Rabin, Begin and Peres

Refugee camps, Jericho

A Druze from Daliyat el Karmil

'Centre Bus Station', Tel Aviv

Fishing nets, the
port of Old Jaffa